Learning your ABC's of Nutrition

Caroline A. Glyman   illustrated by Dee Biser

FOREST HOUSE ™

Forest House Publishing Company, Inc.
Lake Forest, Illinois

FOREST HOUSE ™
Copyright 1992 text by Caroline A. Glyman
Copyright 1992 art by Dee Biser
All rights reserved

No part of this publication may be reproduced, stored in a retrieval system, or transmitted, in any form or by any means, electronic, mechanical, photocopying, recording, or otherwise, without the prior written permission of the publisher.

Layout and design by Kathryn Schoenick

Published by Forest House Publishing Co., Inc,
P. O. Box 738
Lake Forest, Illinois 60045

Printed and bound in the United States of America.
1 2 3 4 5 6 7 8 9 R 01 00 99 98 97 96 95 94 93 92

ISBN 1-878363-75-1

Library of Congress Cataloging-in-Publication Data

Glyman, Caroline A., 1967-
    Learning your ABC's of nutrition / Caroline A. Glyman; illustrated by Dee Biser.
        p.   cm.
    Includes index.
    Summary: Rhyming text discusses vitamins A to E and their importance in good nutrition.
    ISBN 1-878363-75-1
    1. Nutrition--Juvenile literature. [1. Vitamins. 2. Nutrition.]
I. Biser, Dee, ill. II. Title.
QP141.G56 1992
613.2--dc20
                                                         92-7862
                                                              CIP
                                                               AC

CONSULTANT

EDYE WAGNER, R.D., Chief Clinical Dietitian,
Lake Forest Hospital, Lake Forest, Illinois

There are many vitamins in the foods you know,
that keep you healthy from head to toe.

From vitamin **A** to vitamin **E**,
we will learn our vitamin **A, B, C**'s.

Vitamin **A** helps you to see
when it is light, or dark as can be.

Vitamin **A** helps your organs and skin,
so they will be healthy outside and in.

Vitamin **A** helps your organs stay strong,
so infections can't harm them or last very long.

It is found in broccoli, carrots, and cantaloupe too,
plus spinach and liver to name a few.

Apricots, peaches, and milk have **A**, and so do the eggs that chickens lay.

There are many kinds of vitamin **B**.
Most of them give you energy.

They are needed by your nerve cells too,
which tell your body what to do.

If you have a hard day and feel nervous or fearful,
some extra **B**'s can keep you more cheerful.

They help you think in a positive way, so get enough of them every day.

Vitamin **B**'s are in liver and meat,
in nuts and milk and eggs you can eat.

Cheese, chicken and fish have a lot,
so serve them up tasty and hot.

Vitamin *C* helps your wounds heal fast.
It fights infections so they will not last.

It keeps blood flowing so it will not clot
and prevents your body from bruising a lot.

Vitamin *C*, you have been told,
might help you cure a common cold.

Oranges, grapefruits, green peppers, tomatoes,
have vitamin **C,** as well as potatoes.

Berries and brussels sprouts have **C**
and leafy green vegetables like broccoli.

Fruit juice, spinach and cauliflower too,
are sources of **C** that are good for you.

Vitamin **D** builds strong teeth and bone
and keeps them strong when you are grown.

The sun has a vitamin just for you.
It shines through wind and weather, too.

Vitamin **D** comes from the sun.
The skin soaks it up on everyone.

Milk and dairy foods have a supply,
if the sun is not shining in the sky.

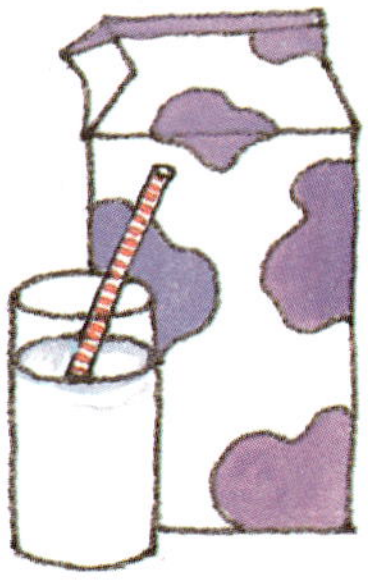

Tuna and salmon have vitamin **D**
and so do other fish that swim in the sea.

Vitamin *E* is good for your skin, keeping it healthy outside and in.

Vitamin **E** gives you strength to shout and run and play and not tire out.

Vitamin *E* fills you with pep
and puts an extra spring in your step.

It can help heal burns and blood clots too,
as fresh blood flows inside of you.

Along with the others, *E* and *A* may keep you well on a gray, rainy day.

Whole grain cereals have vitamin **E** and so do nuts and broccoli.

Eggs and walnuts and sunflower seeds can help you get these vitamin needs.

Leafy green vegetables, spinach and sprouts, have vitamin *E*, without any doubts.

There are many more vitamins than **A** through **E**,
in foods that are good for you and me.

We have only named a famous few,
but all of them are good for you.

The vitamins in food are important to know,
because these vitamins will help you to grow.

They will help you think, smile and run,
so spread the word to everyone.

INDEX

VITAMIN	SOURCES
VITAMIN *A*	broccoli, carrots, cantaloupe, spinach, liver, apricots, peaches, milk, eggs
VITAMIN *B*	liver, meat, nuts, eggs, milk, cheese, chicken, fish
VITAMIN *C*	oranges, grapefruits, berries, fruit juice, tomatoes, potatoes, green vegetables, cauliflower
VITAMIN *D*	sun, milk, dairy foods, tuna, salmon, fish
VITAMIN *E*	whole grain cereals, nuts, eggs, sunflower seeds, green vegetables

ABOUT THE AUTHOR

CAROLINE GLYMAN was born and raised in Lake Forest, Illinois. In 1989, she graduated Magna Cum Laude from the University of Illinois, earning her degree in English Literature. Her first three published children's books are: *Learning Your ABC's of Nutrition, What's Above the Sky: A BOOK ABOUT THE PLANETS,* and *The Birthday Present*. This new and exciting author's goal is to encourage children to develop a positive self-image and an imagination, which she says, "are the most important parts of themselves."

ABOUT THE ILLUSTRATOR

DEE BISER currently lives in Madison, Wisconsin. Dee received her BFA and MA from Northern Illinois University, and was a pre-school teacher prior to illustrating children's books. As a former teacher, Dee understands and makes use of engaging bright colors and characters to express the message of her books. She hopes her unique illustrations will help "open a door" of imagination in each reader's own mind.